SUNDAY MORNING LIVE

VOLUME 5

Willow Creek Resources™ is a publishing partnership between Zondervan Publishing House and the Willow Creek Association. Willow Creek Resources™ includes drama sketches, small group curricula, training material, videos, and many other specialized ministry resources.

Willow Creek Association is an international network of churches ministering to the unchurched. Founded in 1992, the Willow Creek Association serves churches through conferences, seminars, regional roundtables, consulting, and ministry resource materials. The mission of the Association is to assist churches in reestablishing the priority and practice of reaching lost people for Christ through church ministries targeted to seekers.

For conference and seminar information please write to:

Willow Creek Association
P.O. Box 3188
Barrington, Illinois 60011-3188

SUNDAY MORNING LIVE

VOLUME 5

A Collection of Drama Sketches from Willow Creek Community Church

Edited by Steve Pederson

ZondervanPublishingHouse
Grand Rapids, Michigan
A Division of HarperCollins*Publishers*

Sunday Morning Live: Volume 5
Copyright © 1993 by Willow Creek Association
All rights reserved

Requests for information should be addressed to:
Zondervan Publishing House
Grand Rapids, Michigan 49530

Library of Congress Cataloging-in-Publication Data

Sunday morning live.
    1. Christian drama, American. I. Pederson, Steve.
II. Willow Creek Community Church (South Barrington, Ill.)
PS627.R4S8   1993   812'.54080382   92-26029
ISBN 0-310-59221-6 (v. 1)
ISBN 0-310-61361-2 (v. 2)
ISBN 0-310-61441-4 (v. 3)
ISBN 0-310-61531-3 (v. 4)
ISBN 0-310-61541-0 (v. 5)

Cover design by Cheryl Van Andel

Printed in the United States of America

93 94 95 96 97 98 / ❖ CH / 10 9 8 7 6 5 4 3 2 1

To the entire Programming Team
at Willow Creek Community Church:

As a result of your input, critiques, and companionship, not
only is our writing positively affected, but our lives as well.

"We came together to do corporately
what none of us can do alone."

Contents

About the Contributors

Donna Hinkle Lagerquist has been a part of the Willow Creek drama team for twelve years and a writer for five. Her sketch *Stolen Jesus* has recently been adapted into a Canadian Television Christmas special. Donna and her husband, Paul, and their daughter, Carly, live in Cary, Illinois.

Judson Poling was drama director at Willow Creek for five years. He continues to serve on Willow Creek's staff in the area of small group leadership training. Judson is also co-author of the *Walking With God Series,* Willow Creek's small group curriculum. Judson holds a Master of Divinity degree from Trinity Evangelical Divinity School. He lives with his wife, Debra, and their two children in Algonquin, Illinois.

Sharon Sherbondy has been a member of the drama team for fifteen years and a writer for nine. Her drama ministry has taken her throughout the United States and abroad. She is co-author of *Super Sketches for Youth Groups,* a finalist for the Gold Medallion Book Award. Sharon home schools her two children and lives with her husband, Steve, in Elgin, Illinois.

Introduction

In 1975, Willow Creek Community Church began in a rented movie theater in suburban Chicago. Founded with the expressed purpose of reaching the nonchurched, today Willow Creek attracts upwards of 15,000 people to its weekend "seeker services."

Since the beginning, drama has been an integral part of Willow Creek's outreach. Different from traditional church drama, these sketches are short, six- to eight-minute, contemporary vignettes, rooted in real-life experience. Today many churches all over the country, both large and small, are using these sketches as a powerful part of their ministry.

The Message "Set Up"

These sketches are not intended to stand on their own. Rather, they are used to create interest in an issue by grabbing the attention of the audience and getting them to identify with the characters. Also, the sketches do not provide easy answers, but instead raise questions, which the pastor then seeks to answer in the message. Much of the material in this volume may seem "secular," in that there is no specific "Christian" content in the sketch itself. For example, *Check Mates* explores in a comical fashion the periodic checkbook balancing routine that most couples dread. While eventually Rob and Judy both claim some responsibility for their financial mismanagement, they end up unable to take any action which could help remedy the situation. The sketch offers no answer for the mess they find themselves in. However, when performed in connection with a message that presents biblical principles of financial management, the sketch takes on spiritual significance.

This separation of drama and message is a major difference between Willow Creek's approach to drama and that traditionally taken by many churches. While difficult for some people to accept, such a separation is supported by dramatic tradition throughout history. Dorothy Sayers, Christian playwright and novelist, summed it up well: "Playwrights are not evangelists." A dictum frequently repeated to aspiring playwrights is "if you have a message, send it through Western Union." At Willow Creek we try not to abuse drama as an art form by manipulating it to preach a message. Simply put, the sketches clarify the "bad news" so the pastor can bring the "good news."

The Audience "Set Up"

A sketch cannot "set up" a message if viewers do not, in some way, see themselves mirrored in the action. Drama works because people experience vicariously what characters act out on stage. We want to engage not only the minds, but also the emotions of our audience. And drama, which results in high identification, appeals to people's hearts as well as their heads.

At Willow Creek we use contemporary "slice of life" drama, rather than enacted biblical stories, because people more readily identify with characters who act and talk like they do and who confront the same daily issues. This approach helps us earn the right to be heard, because our seekers realize that the church is in touch with the real world, where real people live, work, and struggle.

The sketch *Wait Until Halftime* revolves around a "non-churched Harry" character who has no interest in spiritual matters. His wife, on the other hand, is a spiritual seeker who has difficulty understanding her husband's total disinterest. Their conflict is comically and somewhat poignantly explored, but there is no resolution. At the end of the sketch both characters end up on opposite ends of the issue, just as they were at the beginning. Hopefully, however, their tension has been honestly played out.

We've discovered that the degree of audience identification directly parallels what we call the "reality factor." Drama earns credibility with an audience when it is honest and truthful in how it handles material. If drama comes off as simplistic and naïve, or presents clichéd, easy answers, it will not produce the desired result.

Because I Love You depicts, in a very straightforward manner, the damage and pain that can result in a marriage when trust has been broken through infidelity. The sketch is stark and honest and therefore might be avoided by some churches. But if we shy away from such real-life issues, or too easily resolve the conflict, we will undermine the reality factor as well as greatly diminish drama's potential to impact an audience.

If drama is to be optimally effective in the church, we must be passionately committed to being real, warts and all. We need to avoid easy answers, because they ultimately don't help, even if they sound good. Seekers and believers alike want truth, not a sugarcoated, sanitized version of reality.

In his book *Open Windows,* in a chapter entitled "Pitfalls of Christian Writing," Philip Yancey laments:

> Sometimes when I read Christian books, especially in the fields of fiction and biography, I have a suspicion that characters have been strangely lobotomized. . . . Just as a lobotomy flattens out emotional peaks and valleys, Christian writers can tend to safely reduce life's tensions and strains to a more acceptable level. . . . A perverse fear of overstatement keeps us confined to that flatland realm of "safe" emotions and tensions—a fear that seems incredible in light of the biblical model.

The cause of Christ would be well served if the church would listen to Yancey. For it is truth-telling (which isn't very safe) that not only gives ministry integrity, but also opens up seekers to the possibility of transformation through the power of the gospel.

Getting Started

The sketch format is a fairly easy way for any church, regardless of size, to begin using drama. A little time, a few simple props, a couple of actors (in some cases just one), and a director are all the necessary elements.

Because sketches are short, the time demand for rehearsals is not excessive. Typically, we spend about four to five hours rehearsing each one. If you are working with relatively inexperienced people, however, it would probably be wise to plan more time. Our four hours is divided into two rehearsals. The actors pick up their scripts one week before the performance. Our first rehearsal is early in the week, during which time we discuss the characters and work out the basic movement (blocking). Because we have only two rehearsals, we ask the actors to memorize the script prior to this rehearsal, with the goal of being off the script by the end of the two-hour session.

For the second rehearsal—in our case, before it is performed for the first service—we rehearse one and a half hours, working on stage with the hand props and furniture we'll be using. During this time we polish the movement, work on character consistency, pacing, and the rise

and fall of the action. If movement doesn't look natural because an actor is having a hard time making it look motivated, we change it. After we're off the stage, we run lines or work problem areas of blocking for an additional half to full hour. We also try to relax and enjoy each other's company before the service begins.

For props, we use only that which is absolutely necessary. In other words, we don't use furniture to establish setting unless it fulfills a necessary function in the sketch. If, for example, a phone is needed, we would use an end table to set it on. But if nothing needs to sit on the end table, why use one? Typically we do not use door or window units. If a window is called for, we mime it. However, rather than mime the opening and closing of an imaginary door, which gets cumbersome, the actors simply enter a room, a convention which audiences seem to accept.

A simple rule of thumb for props and scenic pieces is to use only what is necessary, keeping them simple and relying on the audience's imagination to fill in the details. Not only is this an easier route, but—unless you have a professional set designer—it is also the most effective. Furthermore, since props usually need to be set in place before a sketch and removed afterwards, the simpler you can keep it, the better.

While the technical elements necessary to produce a good sketch are fairly basic, assembling the right actors and someone to "lead the charge" might prove more challenging. Talent in drama, unlike the other arts, is somewhat difficult to assess quickly. If someone cannot sing a song or play an instrument, it is readily evident, but acting talent is more difficult to define. To further complicate the matter, drama seems to attract people who have an affinity for the arts but who lack specific talent or training. Someone reasons, "I can't sing, or play the piano, but I think I can act." Indeed, maybe this person has acting ability, but too often such people are drawn to drama because it appears relatively "easy," at least compared to the other arts. But doing drama well is more difficult than it appears. Unfortunately, many well-intentioned people, because they know little about the craft of drama, have not helped further the cause of drama in the church. God is not served when drama is done poorly.

Therefore, before getting serious about drama, even short sketches, the church must find a competent drama director. This person needs to have adequate people skills, the ability to assess acting talent, and an understanding of the basics of stage direction. If someone possesses great drama instincts but lacks formal training, it would be a wise investment for a church to enroll this person in some courses in acting and directing at a local college. A good course in directing can provide many of the basic principles necessary for staging drama effectively.

Having formally trained actors is an advantage, but most churches do not have this luxury—all the more reason to have someone with skill and training leading the team. Over time, talented lay people with good dramatic instincts can develop into strong performers, even if they have no previous drama experience, but their growth will be severely limited if their directors do not have sufficient training.

And finally, a word of encouragement. Once a person has understood some basic principles of theatre—as simple as this sounds—that person learns to do drama by *doing* drama. Even the most inexperienced actors and directors can improve, as long as they are willing to learn from their mistakes.

Throughout our many years of doing drama at Willow Creek, we have made numerous mistakes. We still do. In the earlier years, for example, too many of our scripts were "preachy," and therefore stilted and manipulated. Today, periodically, we do a script that we think will work, but it ends up falling flat, due to a lack of conflict, identification, humor, or any number of factors. Sometimes it is particularly frustrating because it's difficult to figure out exactly why a script appeared not to "go over." Such is the business of doing original drama. But as long as we try to learn from each experience, over time we improve the quality and increase our understanding of the craft of drama.

It is our hope that the "tested" resources in *Sunday Morning Live Volume 5,* and others in volumes 1, 2, 3 and 4, will provide you with at least one of the necessary elements for doing drama—the script.

Based on our experience at Willow Creek, these sketches have worked well. We pray they will work well for you, too.

Steve Pederson
Drama Director
Willow Creek
    Community Church

Because
I Love You

Michelle has planned a romantic dinner for her husband, Eric, only to have it spoiled when he picks up a piece of junk mail. How could one simple letter—a mere envelope in this case—undo Eric so quickly? We discover that Michelle had an affair four years earlier with a man who worked at the company which sent the letter. Suddenly, the romantic evening turns cold. Michelle and Eric argue, and Eric reveals his deep wounds and continued lack of trust, even after four years. The sketch ends with the couple alienated and hurting.

TOPICS: adultery, marriage, forgiveness, lasting consequences of sin

CHARACTERS:

Michelle a wife who is trying to convince her husband of her faithfulness

Eric a husband who has difficulty trusting his wife

PROPS: table set for two, chair, end table, stack of mail

Because I Love You

Sharon Sherbondy

Setting: *Michelle is lighting the candles at a dining room table set for two. An overstuffed chair and an end table are to the side. Eric enters, having been at the office. Although the scene is written with a romantic tone, Michelle and Eric are almost too nice to each other, as if they are putting their best foot forward.*

Eric: *(entering)* Hi.

Michelle: Hi. Well, you're right on time.

Eric: Aren't I usually?

Michelle: Yeah, I guess you are.

Eric: So what's the occasion?

Michelle: We're celebrating the fact that none of our children are home.

Eric: Bad day, huh?

Michelle: The worst.

Eric: Well, had I known all this was waiting for me, I would have cut out of the meeting even earlier.

Michelle: What meeting was that?

Eric: Oh, with some of our new clients.

Michelle: Eric, why didn't you tell me? We could have done this another time.

Eric: No. That's okay.

Michelle: Eric!

Eric: Michelle, it's fine, really.

Michelle: Well, since you're here, I suppose we should eat. Are you hungry?

Eric: Uh, yeah.

Michelle: *(pause)* This didn't happen to be another one of those early dinner meetings, was it?

Eric: Well, they ate, I didn't.

Michelle: Eric . . .

Eric: Michelle, it's fine. I don't eat at those things. My goal is to wine and dine *them*. So, what are we having?

Michelle: Beef Wellington.

Eric: Wow!

Michelle: Oh, Honey, that's just the beginning. So why don't you make yourself comfortable while I finish up here? *(She puts finishing touches on the table.)*

Eric: There's an offer I can't refuse. *(He sits and picks up the mail.)* I've been waiting for that letter from Jim Hartman, but . . . *(He stops suddenly, looking at a letter. His face hardens.)*

Michelle: *(not noticing his reaction, looking at her watch)* Well, just a few minutes longer. How 'bout if I get you something to drink?

Eric: *(coldly)* No thanks.

Michelle: Are you sure? *(He doesn't respond.)* Eric?

(After a fairly long pause he passes an envelope to her over his shoulder. She looks at it.)

Eric: So that's what this little charade of yours is all about.

Michelle: Eric, I had no idea this was here. I haven't looked at the mail yet.

Eric: You expect me to believe that?

Michelle: It's a label, Eric. My name must be on a mailing list.

Eric: So why don't you open it?

Michelle: There's nothing personal about it.

Eric: Open it.

Michelle: You've got to be kidding.

Eric: Open it!

Michelle: *(tears it open)* It's just an advertisement! Here, look at it!

Eric: I don't want to look at it.

Michelle: I swear, Eric. I didn't know it was here. Believe me, if I had, I would have thrown it out.

Eric: Thrown it out? How many others have you thrown out?

Michelle: *(trying to be calm)* Eric, please don't do this. Please.

Eric: What would you like me to do, forget it ever happened?

Michelle: Eric, I have not heard nor do I want to hear from John.

Eric: *(crossing away)* Don't say his name.

Michelle: It's a stupid form letter, Eric, and he probably doesn't even work there anymore. My gosh, it's been years. *(pause)* This is not fair.

Eric: You're talking to me about what's fair. Because of you, I'm barely keeping my head above water at work. While everybody else is working their tail off bringing in new business, I'm rushing home to my wife.

Michelle: Eric . . .

Eric: Because if I don't, she might just . . .

Michelle: Have an affair? Eric, that's not going to happen.

Eric: That's what I used to think.

Michelle: What's it going to take? What do I have to do to prove to you that I was wrong, it was a mistake, and that it will never happen again?

Eric: I don't know.

Michelle: *(pause)* Do you realize I have no friends? I even quit going out with my girlfriends for fear that you'll think I'm . . . *(harshly)* sleeping around. *(pause)* Four years. Four years, Eric. How much more time do you need before you can forget it, and let us get on with our lives?

Eric: Four years. Yeah, four years. And how do I know there haven't been others?

Michelle: Not this again. We get some stupid form letter and suddenly I'm a two-bit tramp sleeping with every guy in town!

Eric: Stop it! *(crossing away)*

Michelle: *(spinning him around, very angry)* No, you stop it! It's over, Eric. It's done.

It'll never happen again. Now please, will you just let it go.

Eric: I can't. *(painfully)* I'm trying. Believe me, I'm trying. But I can't.

Michelle: *(looks at him with hurt and anger)* Then leave. *(Eric turns away. She is on the verge of tears.)* Why do you stay? If you're so . . . unsure of me, why do you stay?

Eric: *(looking at her)* Because I love you! *(Michelle puts her head down, broken. Eric turns away.)*

Fadeout

Prayer Group Therapy

Four would-be "pray-ers" meet for group therapy. In this case, each member has some sort of common prayer dysfunction. Doug is compulsive about his "holy language," and his prayers are full of outbursts and "hallelujahs" that disrupt the others. Margaret uses prayer as a vehicle for gossip. Pam is timid and uses only memorized or formula prayers. Joe doesn't really pray at all because he has concluded that God knows everything—so why pray? Karen, the facilitator, tries to get everyone to participate in a simple time of prayer, but as each person's warped perspective on prayer kicks in, the results are disastrous—in an outlandishly comical way!

TOPICS: Prayer

CHARACTERS:

Doug	an overenthusiastic pray-er
Margaret	a gossipy pray-er
Pam	a timid pray-er
Joe	a skeptical pray-er
Karen	the facilitator

PROPS: five chairs

Prayer Group Therapy

Donna Hinkle Lagerquist

Setting: *Five chairs in a semicircle.*

Karen: Okay, I think it's time for us to begin. Why don't we all have a seat? Wherever you feel comfortable. Now, I'm sure some of you are a bit uneasy. I know it seems unusual to have group therapy on prayer, but since so many people struggle in this area, I thought it would be good to give it a try. So, why don't we start by going around the circle and giving our names and saying why we are here? I'll start. My name is Karen, and I'm here to help facilitate this group and hopefully help you all to a happy, healthy prayer life.

Doug: I'm Brother Doug. And I'm here because the members of my blessed Bible study sent me. Praise the Lord!

Karen: Do you know why they sent you here, Doug?

Doug: I'm not sure, Sister Karen, but I believe, yes I do believe, hallelujah, amen, I believe it had something to do with grandstanding and interrupting our times together, our blessed times of prayer.

Karen: Okay. Good sharing, Doug. Thanks.

Doug: To God be the glory, not me.

Karen: Thanks, Doug.

Doug: Hallelujah.

Karen: Next?

Doug: Praise Jesus!

Karen: *(quickly)* Thanks, Doug. Next?

Margaret: Well, my name is Margaret, and I'm not one to gossip, but I'm here because someone, who shall remain nameless, thought I needed it. But then, Evelyn Rathby is always sticking her nose into other people's business.

Doug: Thank you, Jesus.

Margaret: *(a bit taken aback by Doug)* Anyway, I'm here.

Karen: All right, let's keep moving around the circle.

Pam: *(very nervous, reading from 3 x 5 card)* Hello, my name is . . . Pam, and I'm here because I have difficulty with expressing myself.

Karen: We're certainly glad you're here, Pam. Next?

Joe: I'm Joe.

Karen: And why are you here, Joe?

Joe: *(flippantly)* God knows.

Karen: Would you mind sharing what you mean with the rest of the group?

Joe: The way I look at it, God knows exactly what I'm thinking, so I'm not sure I understand what the purpose of praying is. If God knows what I'm going to say before I say it, why bother saying it?

Karen: Well, I hope by being here you'll feel free to join in. *(now addressing everyone)* Remember, prayer is talking to God. Now, what we are going to do is start out with an open group prayer. This is where you jump in whenever you feel led. *(Doug is getting all revved up.)* Keep it short. I won't interrupt this time. It will be sort of a trial run to get a feel for where all of us are at. Okay, you can bow your heads or close your eyes . . . whatever you need to do to feel comfortable . . . and let's begin. *(Doug gets on his knees; Pam pulls out an index card.)*

Doug: *(very dramatic)* Oh, most holy God, Father God, we beseech thee oh Lord, Father, God, amen, hallelujah, amen. Lord God, hear our prayers this day. Amen, praise you, Lord. Amen. Amen!

Margaret: *(under breath)* Oh, dear. *(normal voice)* Dear God, thank you for this time to be together. It is so nice to be here with people who care. There are so many out there who don't . . .

Pam: *(thinking she's done)* God . . .

Margaret: Like Libby Johnson. Now Lord, you know that I'm not one to gossip, Lord, but I overheard her the

other day telling the cashier at Dominicks that she would have an affair with the first man that came along, just to spite her husband for working so many hours overtime. And let me tell you, Lord . . . with the little skimpy skirt and sweater she had on, I was sure the produce man would have gone for her . . .

Karen: Margaret . . .

Margaret: *(on a roll)* Except of course that he's been divorced twice and his third wife would probably kill him.

Karen: Margaret, keep it short.

Margaret: Amen.

Doug: Yes, Lord!

Pam: *(painfully shy, hesitant)* God . . .

Doug: Amen!

Pam: God . . .

Doug: Hallelujah!

Pam: *(quickly to prohibit Doug from jumping in)* God grant us the serenity to . . . *(realizes Doug hasn't jumped in, but is still very uneasy)* accept the things I cannot . . . change . . . *(painfully slow)* and the courage to change the things I can . . . and the wis . . . wis . . . *(All group members are leaning in trying to speed her up.)*

Joe: *(can't wait anymore)* The wisdom to know the difference!

Doug: Thank you, Jesus!

Karen: All right, all right, let's stop for a little analysis here. First, I want to remind you all that prayer is just talking to God. Like we would to a friend. He wants to know what you're feeling—what you're concerned about. It's as simple as that, all right? Now then, Pam . . .

Pam: *(panics)* What?

Karen: *(gently)* I'd like you to be a little more spontaneous. Tell God how you're feeling and try using your own words.

Pam: Okay, I'll try.

Karen: And Doug, buddy. Doug, Doug, Doug, you only have to say God's name once. He has great hearing. Okay? *(gently)* And could you try to keep your comments to yourself?

Margaret: Amen to that!

Doug: Well, Sister, I think your comments about the produce man and the like are also a distraction to the holy avenue of prayer.

Margaret: *(jumping up)* Who do you think you are criticizing the way that I pray?

Doug: *(also getting up)* Sister, I discern a very evil spirit lurking deep down inside . . .

Karen: Okay, okay, okay—have a seat. Now then, everyone, we are here to help one another! *(trying to rescue the situation)* We're going to try this once again, and Joe, please feel free to jump in at any time!

Doug: Oh, most holy God, Father God, we beseech thee, oh Lord!

Karen: Doug, just say his name once!

Margaret: Lord, some people in this group have really big mouths . . .

Doug: God! You rested on the seventh day. May some here tonight learn how to rest their opinions . . .

Pam: "Deliver us from evil."

Doug: Praise the Lord!

Margaret: Lord, shut some people's mouths so others might speak!

Doug: Lord, out of thy merciful compassion, stuff her mouth!

Joe: *Ahhhhhh!* God, get me out of here!

Karen: Oh, Joe, Joe, that was excellent! See, prayer is just telling God what's on your heart.

Doug: *Amen! (Karen, having had enough from Doug, pushes him over in his chair.)*

Karen & Joe: (*"high-fiving" each other*) Hallelujah!

Blackout

Wait Until Halftime

Larry is into watching his basketball game when Beth comes in to suggest they do something more social for the evening. When she proposes inviting over another couple, Craig and Robin, he becomes especially disinterested. While she finds them interesting, caring people, he doesn't like their Christianity. The exchange is mostly light-hearted until the end, when she expresses concern for his eternal well-being. He quips about burial in "asbestos underwear" to try to fend her off. In his mind, eternity can "wait until halftime."

TOPICS: evangelism, heaven and hell

CHARACTERS:

    Larry   an easy-going nonbeliever
    Beth   a spiritual seeker

PROPS: couch, end table with drawer, various books, tapes, etc., remote control

Wait Until Halftime

Sharon Sherbondy

Setting: *Larry is sitting on a couch, remote control in hand, watching a basketball game on TV. He's very focused on the game.*

Beth: *(entering)* So, what do you want to do tonight?

Larry: I don't care.

Beth: Do you want to go out?

Larry: No.

Beth: Rent a movie?

Larry: No.

Beth: Play cards?

Larry: No.

Beth: Well, what do you want to do?

Larry: *(preoccupied)* I don't care, but would you mind talking about it in another room?

Beth: Come on, Larry, it's Friday night.

Larry: I'm trying to watch the game.

Beth: I don't want to watch basketball. Come on, let's go see a movie.

Larry: I don't want to go to a movie.

Beth: *(picks up paper)* Let's just see what's playing. *(brief pause)* Will you look at this, more news on Clinton. Clinton this, Clinton that, Clinton, Clinton, Clinton. Honey, how do you think Clinton's doing so far?

Larry: *(irritated with all her talking)* I think Hillary's doing just fine.

Beth: At least Bill listens to his wife. Oh look, *(name a current movie)* just opened.

Larry: Beth, Honey. *(hands her the phone)*

Beth: What?

Larry: I want you to call somebody.

Beth: *(confused)* Who?

Larry: Anybody, so you can talk to them and I can watch my game.

Beth: Is that all you care about, your stupid sport's channel?

Larry: *(responding to a play on TV)* Yes!

Beth: Okay. Okay. I'll call somebody. Somebody who enjoys the art of conversation. *(Gets an idea, begins dialing.*

Larry has a quick realization and presses down the receiver.) Hey, what are you doing?

Larry: You are not calling Craig and Robin.

Beth: Why not?

Larry: I promise . . . I'll talk to you at halftime.

Beth: *(knowing better)* No, you won't. Look, you and Craig can watch the game together, and Robin and I will sit and talk.

Larry: Wrong. You and Robin will talk, then pretty soon Craig will join in, and then I'm dragged into it . . .

Beth: Have you or have you not always had a good time with Craig?

Larry: Yes. But do we have to talk about this now?

Beth: Yes. *(She grabs remote and turns off the TV.)*

Larry: *(very frustrated)* I just want to relax and enjoy the game.

Beth: So tell me, why don't you want them over here?

Larry: *(defensive)* I can't be myself when they're around.

Beth: You mean you can't swear at the ref.

Larry: Well, it's important during a big game.

Beth: They've never said a word about your language.

Larry: They're thinking about it though. Why else would they keep asking us to church?

Beth: Keep asking us to church?! Where's this coming from? They've asked maybe three times in two years.

Larry: Yeah, but it's always coming up.

Beth: What? Church?

Larry: The church thing isn't so bad. It's the other stuff that goes along with it.

Beth: They have never forced their beliefs on us.

Larry: No, just their propaganda. Every time they come over they bring something for us either to read or listen to or watch.

Beth: Because I ask for it. They bring it for me. I happen to find this topic very interesting, and I want to know more about it.

Larry: Well, they bring it in by the truckload.

Beth: You're exaggerating.

Larry: Oh, I am? Have you looked at all this stuff they've given us? *(pulls out drawer in the end table and dumps the contents on the floor)* We got pamphlets, we got books, Bibles, tapes, tape series, more books, movies, invitations to church things.

Beth: So they're resourceful people.

Larry: *(reads some off quickly with a build to the last line) The Bridge, Was Jesus Christ God's Son, Is the Bible True, Evidence*

That Demands a Verdict, More Evidence That Demands a Verdict, The Life of Christ, The Case for Christ, The Credibility of Christ? These people need to broaden their interests!

Beth: It's important to them.

Larry: *(crossing back to sofa)* Well, basketball's important to me, but that doesn't mean I have to read every sports magazine in print.

Beth: *(crossing to pick up the books)* That would require turning off the TV. *(short pause)* Larry, have you even bothered looking at any of this?

Larry: As a matter of fact, I have.

Beth: And?

Larry: And it's very . . . thorough.

Beth: Well, what do you think?

Larry: I think it's fine . . . for them.

Beth: What if there's more to it?

Larry: And so what if there is? Beth, I'm perfectly happy with the way things are.

Beth: Maybe things could be better. Is that possible?

Larry: How? We're comfortable, we've got a nice home, we've got everything we could possibly want, except maybe a quiet place to watch the game.

Beth: Did you ever consider that there's more to life than basketball?

Larry: No. *(noticing she's upset)* Yes, of course. I'm kidding. Beth, where's your sense of humor?

Beth: I'm not so sure this is funny stuff, Larry. There's some other things at stake here.

Larry: Oh?

Beth: You know, like heaven and . . .

Larry: *(sarcastic)* Hell?

Beth: Well, yeah.

Larry: So bury me in asbestos underwear.

Beth: *(frustrated)* Larry, you don't take anything seriously.

Larry: Well, for the next few minutes I want to do some heavy bonding with MJ, Scotty, and the boys in red. *(Insert your local sports heroes and team color.)* We can deal with eternity at halftime. *(turns TV back on)*

Fadeout

Family Values

Paula and her mom meet after what appears to have been a long separation. Her mother wants her to come home, but Paula indicates she wants to stay. It is soon apparent Paula has joined some kind of cult. As Mom describes the life she wants Paula to come home to, her "party-hearty" brother and Mom's on-again, off-again romance, it becomes obvious why Paula left in the first place. The brainwashing of the cult seems tragic, but the group's apocalyptic message clearly appeals to Paula's idealism. A member of the group enters to escort Paula back. She decides to leave with him, and Mom is left calling for her daughter in an empty room.

TOPICS: cults, broken families, the need to belong

CHARACTERS:
> **Mom** a divorced, middle-aged woman
> **Paula** an idealistic young woman
> **Man** a member of the cult

PROPS: a bench or chairs

Family Values

Judson Poling

Setting: *Scene opens on Mom, a middle-aged woman in some sort of lobby, obviously nervous. Enter Paula, a young adult woman.*

Paula: Mom?

Mom: Paula! *(runs and embraces her)* Oh, Paula, it's so good to see you. *(embraces her again; Paula is not too responsive; Mom steps back and looks at her)* Let me look at you. Well, I'm glad you've still got some meat on your bones. I half expected to see you emaciated.

Paula: This isn't a prison camp, Mom.

Mom: Well, I've read about what happens to people who join groups like this. Sometimes they're not allowed to eat, or go to the bathroom . . .

Paula: You can't believe everything you read.

Mom: No, I suppose you can't . . . *(awkward pause)*

Paula: *(unenthusiastic)* So, how's everything going? How's Ryan?

Mom: Oh, fine. Ryan's enjoying having the house to himself since you . . . uh, came here. He constantly has the gang over, you know, "party hearty." I try to get him to clean up the beer cans from the lawn, but I usually end up doing it myself before the neighbors see the mess. I guess it's just a phase. *(pause)* He's so different from you.

Paula: Yeah, we're different . . . *(pause)* Mom, why are you here?

Mom: *(taken aback)* Why am I here? I want to visit my daughter. Something wrong with that?

Paula: No . . . no. *(pause)* So . . . you and Gary still seeing each other?

Mom: Well, we're having some hard times right now. He still insists we should get married soon. I wish he could understand I'm not ready to make it permanent yet. It would be so much easier if you were home. He really respects you. I know you could get through to him. *(sighs)* Paula, isn't it time you come home?

Paula: So this is why you're here. I knew it.

Mom: I want you home, Paula. I'm ready to forgive and forget.

Paula: I have no intention of going home. I like it here.

Mom: But this place is a cult!

Paula: By whose definition? You don't know what goes on here.

Mom: Well, I talked to several ministers about this place. Every one of them told me it sounded suspicious.

Paula: And not one of them has been here. *(new approach, softer)* Mom, I've met God. I've found his people. Jesus said only a few would be ready, and we're the few.

Mom: You're the few? *(exasperated)*

Paula: Yes, the only ones who can truly hear his voice.

Mom: I want you out of here now!

Paula: My spiritual advisor said this is exactly how you'd be. I should've listened to her.

Mom: Spiritual advisor?

Paula: Yes. We all have an advisor, someone to guide and to counsel us. It's how God works to help us make the right decisions.

Mom: You don't need some "kook" advisor here. You've got your family—

Paula: My family?

Mom: Yes, don't you think God wants you to listen to your family? We can help you if you need advice.

Paula: Who do you suggest I go to first: my father, whose only contact with me for sixteen years has been four birthday cards? Or my kid brother, who gets drunk right underneath your nose every weekend? Now there's wise counsel for you.

Mom: Well, you have me.

Paula: Yes. I have you, but within two minutes of getting here, you're talking about needing me to fix what's wrong between you and your boyfriend! You're supposed to be the mom, remember?

Mom: I *confide* in you. I would think you'd see that as love.

Paula: Love is when you give. Love is when you sacrifice for something bigger than your own concerns, when you care for what the whole community needs. *(pause)* See, I finally found love, Mom. Here, with the people God has gathered around his enlightened master.

Mom: What are you talking about—"enlightened master"?

Paula: Our leader, God's seventh prophet for the Last Days. He teaches the Bible like no one I've ever heard.

Mom: What's wrong with our church?

Paula: Mom, all those people say one thing Sunday and live totally different the rest of the week—including me. I was the worst hypocrite.

Mom: They've really got you down on yourself here, don't they?

Paula: No, they care about me, Mom.

Mom: They don't care about you, they brainwash you. They follow you around and control you. You don't even know how miserable you are here.

Paula: *(biting)* Maybe I should go home with you, where I can be certain of it.

(Another cult member enters.)

Man: Paula. Paula, it's time to go.

Mom: *(angry)* What do you mean, time to go? I'm not finished yet.

Man: Paula. *(She moves toward the man.)*

Mom: *(intercepting her)* Look, Paula, I have your car parked out front, you have your own room in your own house waiting for you. Please come home.

Paula: *(pause)* Well, sorry to disappoint you, but a car and a room isn't enough. Not when I've found a family. *(She exits with the cult member.)*

Mom: Paula, don't do this. Paula, you're making a mistake. Paula? *(yelling after her)* Paula!

(After a beat the lights black out.)

Check Mates

The subject of finances strikes fear in the heart of Rob and excitement in his wife, Judy. In the midst of trying to balance their checkbook, they discover that their significant debt is a shared problem. To correct the situation, they decide to get rid of all their credit cards. When they actually try to do it, however, they end up keeping most of the cards and destroying only two. The plastic pretender prevails!

TOPICS: personal finances, debt, self-deceit

CHARACTERS:

> **Rob**　　a big spender
> **Judy**　　Rob's wife, also a big spender

PROPS: table, two chairs, checkbook, bank statement, calculator, pens

Check Mates

Sharon Sherbondy

Setting: *Stage is set with table and chairs. Judy is setting down an adding machine, checkbook, bank statement, paper, pencils, etc.*

Judy: Oh, Rob. Rob. Rob!! *(Rob offstage makes exaggerated coughing and gagging noises.)* Rob? What's wrong?

Rob: *(still offstage, having difficulty talking)* I don't know. It hit me all of a sudden. I think I'll take a nap. *(more coughing)*

Judy: *(She's on to him.)* Robert Miller, you get out here right now. Do you hear me?!

Rob: But, I . . .

Judy: Don't "but" me. Get out here or I'll come in there and drag you out.

Rob: *(enters reluctantly)* All right, all right. I'm coming.

Judy: Now come over here and sit down.

Rob: I don't want to sit down.

Judy: Sit down!

Rob: *(sitting)* All right, if we can just get this over with.

Judy: Honestly, a grown man acting like a two-year-old. You're of check-writing age, so let's get to work. Now, I'll give you the bank statement. You read it off to me, and I'll check it against the checkbook.

Rob: Can't we do this some other time?

Judy: No. First check, please.

Rob: Could we at least take it into the other room so I can watch the game?

Judy: No. First check, please.

Rob: You really get into this dictator stuff, don't you?

Judy: Yes. First check . . .

Rob: Number 1784.

Judy: Number 1784.

Rob: $94.73.

Judy: *(finding it)* Jewel, $94.73. Check. There. See how easy that is?

Rob: So why don't you do it by yourself?

Judy: Because I want to bond with you. Next check, please.

Rob: Well, on the statement it shows a withdrawal of $100.

Judy: What's the date on it?

Rob: August 5.

Judy: I can't seem to find it here.

Rob: Okay. The next check is . . .

Judy: Why do you think that is, *Rob*?

Rob: . . . number 1785.

Judy: Rob?

Rob: I don't know. I must have forgotten to write it down. So sue me.

Judy: *(pauses, frustrated)* What's the next check?

Rob: 1785. $147.32.

Judy: We seem to jump here from 1784 to 1786.

Rob: Oh, really?

Judy: Yes, really. Oh, here it is. After 1793. *(sarcastic)* Of course. And what or who is "Graters"?

Rob: I don't know.

Judy: "I don't know." What do you mean?

Rob: I mean, I don't know. And what makes you think it's mine?

Judy: Because it's illegible.

Rob: I don't remember.

Judy: First, you don't write it down for a week, and then you don't even know what it's for.

Rob: *(angry)* I don't know.

Judy: *(guessing what it could be)* A man . . . a woman . . . an organization . . . a store, a club? What?

Rob: An assassin!

Judy: Go ahead, make jokes. But we're talking about our financial status here.

Rob: Judy, we have plenty of money, okay?

Judy: How would we know with a checkbook that looks like this?

Rob: Judy, that's why there are bank statements, so those people at the bank can keep track. *(She stares at him in disbelief.)* Well, it worked for my folks.

Judy: Right. And that's why they're living with us now.

Rob: Look, according to our checkbook here, *(he glances at it, scowls, then begins flipping through the pages)* we owe money to every major credit card company in the country.

Judy: *(now she's defensive)* That's an exaggeration.

Rob: Visa . . . Mastercard . . . Discover . . . American Express . . .

Judy: Okay.

Rob: J.C. Penney, Sears, Marshall Fields . . .

Judy: All right.

Rob: Spiegel, Lord & Taylor . . .

Judy: *All right!* All right, already! I got it!

Rob: *(growing awareness)* You know, you're absolutely right. Our financial status is at stake.

Judy: Never mind. I'll just do this myself.

Rob: Not a chance. *I'm* suddenly in the mood for some bonding.

Judy: You think these are all my charges?

Rob: I don't shop at Lord & Taylor.

Judy: Where do you think that "favorite" sweater *(gestures to the one he has on)* you're wearing came from? And let's not stop at Lord & Taylor. Here, let's read on. *(She grabs the checkbook.)* We've got The Diner's Club, Ace Hardware, Chicago Health Club, and the Pro Image, the Sharper Image . . .

Rob: *All right!*

Judy: True Value, Handy Andy . . .

Rob: *All right already! (They look at each other, then look away guiltily. After pause)* Okay, so our finances stink!

Judy: Well, there's no creditors knocking at our door—yet.

Rob: Things have gotten a little out of hand.

Judy: Do you know that we probably go through a box of checks a month just paying these bills?

Rob: OK. I got it. Here's what we do. We bring all our credit cards together and we destroy them. *(takes out his billfold)*

Judy: You mean get rid of them?

Rob: *(handing Judy her purse)* Into a hundred pieces.

Judy: And then what? *(She begins taking out many cards.)*

Rob: We go without.

Judy: How are we going to buy stuff?

Rob: We'll write checks.

Judy: Oh, no, you don't. You can't keep track of your checks now, let alone write more of them.

Rob: Okay, okay, then we'll each keep out one credit card. *(He opens billfold and a clear plastic "foldout" drops down loaded with numerous credit cards.)*

Judy: Which one?

Rob: *(looking through his cards)* Well, I'll keep out American Express. I use that when I travel.

Judy: *(looking through her cards)* Okay, I'll keep Master Card. More places accept that.

Rob: *(having second thoughts)* Of course, I should keep my Handy Andy card. You get a five percent discount with every purchase.

Judy: Yeah, and I just got a thing in the mail from Spiegel that they're raising my limit $2000.

Rob: The Pro Shop I should hold on to because I'm going to be needing some new clubs for Florida this winter.

Judy: And Lord & Taylor, Penneys, Marshall Fields—they're all having their fall sales right now.

Rob: And Eddie Bauer is always having sales.

Judy: Okay, so I guess I'll destroy my . . . Philips 66.

Rob: And I'm gonna cut up my . . . Ace Hardware. *(He cuts the card in two.)*

Judy: Great.

Rob: It feels good, doesn't it?

Judy: Yeah, it's great to be in control of our finances. *(She snips her card.)*

Blackout

In . . .
We Trust

In this monologue, a man struggles with trust in the everyday relationships of life. His son has had a recent accident, so he is reluctant to trust his driving. His wife has embarrassed him in front of some coworkers as well as upset his placid marriage with demands he be more sensitive and meet her needs. Every relationship in his life, he confesses, boils down to somebody "using" somebody else, a point with which he bluntly stabs the audience. And then there's trust in God, a whole different subject. Or is it?

TOPICS: trust, difficulty trusting God, father/husband role

CHARACTERS:

Man   a husband and father who has difficulty trusting people

PROPS: chair, end table, magazine

In . . .
We Trust

Judson Poling

Setting: *A man is standing in front of an overstuffed chair with an end table next to it.*

(calling offstage) And I want the car back by eleven . . . yes, I said eleven! *(another thought)* Don't forget to slow down around the turns—it's icy out there. *(with even more emphasis)* And remember to pump your brakes or you'll skid into the guy in front of you! *(under his breath)* Again. *(He sits down, picks up a magazine, and begins looking at it. He stops. Says following to audience.)* Sixteen years ago I thought changing his diapers was a challenge! Now, when I look at that kid behind the wheel of a car, knowing he's got an adult-sized responsibility directed by a teenage-sized brain . . . *(shudders at the thought)* I want to trust him, to believe the best of him, but he's the one who had the accident. Twelve hundred bucks. Well, at least no one got hurt. *(pause)* But it was so stupid. I don't know how many times I've told him, don't follow so closely. He won't listen. It's like everything I say is a call for debate. "What do you mean the world is round, Dad, can you prove it?" He doesn't trust my advice . . . I don't trust his actions. How about that—we do have something in common.

And my wife, she thinks I'm too tough on him. That might be

true some of the time, but not all the time. Besides, her father wasn't even there for her, so I don't know how she can claim to be such an expert. I mean, compared to that man, I'm a regular Ward Cleaver. I guess both of us know what you're not supposed to do, thanks to her folks. I think we're doing a pretty good job with our kids, I mean despite what we're dealing with. *(catches himself)* Look, don't get me wrong or anything—it's nothing major. I mean, all marriages go through stages when one person can't seem to make the other one as "happy" as . . . he thought he used to. But, I'm trying. Meanwhile, she's got her nose buried in some new "psychology" book, which she insists I have to read too. I try to stay open, but let me tell you, I'm not exactly enjoying all these changes in our marriage. I got married to "settle down," like we used to say. My marriage is definitely not doing anything to settle me down.

(long pause) The truth is, it feels more like somebody died, only I haven't been to any funerals. It's like everyone moved away.

They're all still here, but it doesn't feel like it. My wife says I'm not "meeting her needs." *(halfhearted laugh while shaking his head)* Well, what about *my* needs? *(angry)* What does she call embarrassing me in front of everyone at the office party by telling them about the time I— *(stops)* Well, I'm not going to tell her anything in confidence anymore, that's all. You know, "Fool me once, shame on you; fool me twice, shame on me." She wants me to start meeting her needs *(anger)* then maybe she ought to start meeting mine. I take enough crap from the kids and from work. I don't need it from her! *(pause)* I'm trying. But I got a son who won't listen to me, a wife who broadcasts my personal life to anyone who cares to listen, I got friends . . . who seem to like me because of what I can do for them. It's like I don't relate to anybody unless there's some other motive there, you know?

(stepping toward audience) Well, sure you know. 'Cause you all play the game too. You are being used. Yes, you. And you are using other people. Oh,

I know we've got labels to cover it up: "business relation-ships," "friendships" . . . *(pause)* "marriage." And I know I'm not the only one who sees how dark our hearts are. How can we trust anybody, huh?

Yeah, and I can just hear my wife too, "Don't be so cynical." She's right, I suppose. I'm just being honest. I don't trust my son. I'm trying to trust my wife. My friends . . . I wonder if I can trust anybody. I've been around—I'm not stupid. *(almost casually)* I'm not even sure I can trust God, but that's a whole other subject . . . *(pause, reflects)* I think. *(pause)* Anyway, that's how I see it.

Fadeout

Other Willow Creek Resources™ Available

An Inside Look at the Willow Creek Seeker Service Video

An Inside Look at the Willow Creek Worship Service Video

One-on-One with Oliver North Video (an interview with Bill Hybels)

Sunday Morning Live, Volume 1

Sunday Morning Live, Volume 2

Sunday Morning Live, Volume 3

Sunday Morning Live, Volume 4

Sunday Morning Live Video, Volume 1

Sunday Morning Live Video, Volume 2

Sunday Morning Live Video, Volume 3

Sunday Morning Live Video, Volume 4

Sunday Morning Live Video, Volume 5

Walking With God Journal

Walking With God Series

> *Building Your Church*
> *Discovering the Church*
> *"Follow Me!"*
> *Friendship With God*
> *Impacting Your World*
> *The Incomparable Jesus*
> *Leader's Guide 1*
> *Leader's Guide 2*

Individual Drama Sketches Available

A listing and description of the over 200 Willow Creek drama sketches are now available from Willow Creek Resources™. These sketches provide a visually powerful way to introduce and reinforce a variety of biblical topics of interest to seekers and believers alike. Each is written to correspond with a message given by the pastor.

To obtain a free copy of this catalog, or for more information, call 1-800-876-SEEK (7335).